Luciane Guimarães de Paula

Reflective teacher training

Luciane Guimarães de Paula

Reflective teacher training

Considerations on the process of professional development

ScienciaScripts

Imprint

Cover image: Provided by the author

This book is a translation from the original published under ISBN 978-3-330-20443-0.

Publisher:
Sciencia Scripts
is a trademark of
Dodo Books Indian Ocean Ltd. and OmniScriptum S.R.L publishing group

120 High Road, East Finchley, London, N2 9ED, United Kingdom
Str. Armeneasca 28/1, office 1, Chisinau MD-2012, Republic of Moldova, Europe
Printed at: see last page
ISBN: 978-620-8-30119-4

To my husband Toninho, for his love and encouragement in difficult times and for his unconditional support during the realization of my dreams and life projects. To my children Ana Luiza and Davi for being the greatest joy in my life.

ACKNOWLEDGMENTS

To God, for inspiring me and strengthening my steps throughout my academic career.

To my parents, Jacy and Maria Elizia, for their encouragement and unconditional support at every stage of this journey.

To my colleagues and students at UFG, for their support and friendship during difficult times.

Summary

PRESENTATION

This book brings together four chapters that address issues related to the role of reflection in teacher training and in the process of professional development. The book discusses various themes related to teacher training, with special emphasis on the space allocated to reflection in the undergraduate course and in the opportunities for beginning teaching practice.

Chapter 1 describes the emergence of the reflective movement and the dissemination of its theories on the national scene. Roughly speaking, this chapter discusses how reflective education sees the teacher as a researcher of their own practice, as an individual who investigates and creates hypotheses about the events of their classroom practice, rather than just applying the knowledge produced in the academy. It highlights how the reflective teacher not only applies, but constructs knowledge by reflecting on their practice in order to promote their professional development.

The second chapter reflects on how the process of change arises from the teacher's reflection on a problem detected in their practice. In this sense, it is observed that lasting change in teacher behavior is the result of the process of experimenting with new practices and reflecting on their subsequent consequences. In this way, the alternatives that teachers experiment with and reflect on are gradually incorporated into their daily classroom practice.

Chapter 3 discusses the main challenges faced by teachers during the process of teaching and learning a foreign language. It tries to show how reflecting on the problems faced in the classroom and in the school context as a whole can be a way out of the obstacles encountered in everyday school life, especially in the context of public schools. This chapter argues that the first step in dealing with these issues is to conceive of the teaching profession as an eternally unfinished process of formation, since the profession requires a constant process of personal and professional development.

The fourth chapter discusses the opportunities for students to reflect on their practice during their degree course. Firstly, it discusses the students' experience of the classroom during the internship, highlighting some of the shortcomings that have emerged during this very important time for them. The second section of Chapter 4 then describes another opportunity to start practicing in the classroom: teaching foreign languages at the Language Center, an extension project of the Special Academic Unit for Languages and Linguistics at UFG - Catalao Region. In this section, the author describes the activities carried out in the extension project in question, highlighting the importance of reflecting on practice in order to stimulate changes in practice and the professional development of teachers. The third section of this chapter discusses a research project carried out with English language teachers whose aim is precisely to investigate the effects of reflection on the process of professional development of the participating teachers.

The last section, entitled Final thoughts, briefly closes off the issues discussed throughout the four chapters, highlighting, above all, that teacher training courses should encourage teachers to reflect on issues related to classroom practice. It also reiterates the need for teaching professionals to invest in their professional development, since reflective training is, in fact, a process that is constantly under construction.

CHAPTER 1

THE REFLEX MOVEMENT

CHAPTER 1 THE REFLEXIVE MOVEMENT

1.1 Reflective teacher training[1]

Almost a century ago, the first works of what would come to be known as the *Reflexive Movement* appeared on the educational scene, with Dewey's *How We Think* (1959) as a milestone and, soon afterwards, its dissemination in other areas. According to Zeichner and Liston (1996), Dewey was one of the first educational theorists to conceive of teachers as reflective professionals, capable of taking on active roles in curriculum discussions and educational reforms. He was also one of the first scholars to denounce the technical nature of school teaching, which was marked by its isolation and "rupture" with social experiences (DEWEY, 1959, p. 75).

As Dewey argues, one of the main goals of reflective teaching is the need to seek change and development in schools. Dewey's significant contributions concern the nature of thought and concepts such as routine/reflective action and others such as the three steps to reflective action: a) *open-mindedness;* b) *responsibility* and c) *wholeheartedness.*

One of the main people responsible for disseminating Dewey's ideas to other areas was the architect Schon (1983), who based his work on Dewey's ideas in order to value reflection on experience. His work *The reflective practitioner,* published in 1983, presents a critical analysis of the technicist reasoning that dominated his profession until the 20th century and proposes the valorization of practice as a moment of knowledge construction through reflection, analysis and problematization. In addition, he emphasizes the tacit knowledge that is present in the solutions that professionals find to the problems of practice. This tacit, implicit or internalized

[1] This chapter was adapted from chapter 2 of the author's doctoral thesis, defended in 2010 (see references).

knowledge is part of the action, but does not precede it, which implies that reflective practice is valued. According to Ludke (2006, p. 30):

> The enormous spread of Schon's ideas sent a wave throughout the educational community in the direction of the image of a teacher who is more active, critical and autonomous in relation to his or her choices and decisions, as opposed to one who applies ready-made solutions emanating from external spheres, especially those marked with the stamp of technical rationality.

Giroux (1997) developed the concept of the "reflective teacher", so that reflection went beyond what Schon had initially proposed, and began to conceive of the teacher as a "critical intellectual". With this term, according to Contreras (2002), Giroux had the ambition of encompassing three basic assumptions in order to understand the teacher: a) who is an intellectual and not a technical professional; b) who is attentive to critical intellectual practice related to everyday problems; and c) who is not limited to contemplating and understanding the problems detected, but turns to criticizing and transforming social practices in the school context. According to Giroux (1997, p. 157-158), the teacher as critical intellectual must engage in an exercise of self-criticism of the nature and purpose of "teacher preparation, on-the-job training programs and dominant forms of schooling"

Giroux defends the need to develop critical teaching aimed at active citizenship, instead of a conservative pedagogy that emphasizes technique and the passivity of both teacher and student. This author argues that conservative teaching mediated by schools and their traditional curricula, as opposed to the emancipation of education, has legitimized values and attitudes necessary for the maintenance of the dominant society. In a way, this paradigm is reproduced in the classroom, where the dominant academic knowledge is imposed on the teacher's knowledge and the teacher's knowledge is imposed on the student's knowledge, so that school reality mirrors the reality found in society as a whole. Therefore, the practice of the critical reflective teacher serves not only his own emancipation, but also the emancipation of his students.

Giroux (1997) states that teachers need to organize themselves collectively to reflect on the educational context, in order to improve working conditions and demonstrate their fundamental role in school reforms. However, he doesn't make it clear enough how teachers can transform the society around them or actually become a "critical intellectual". Contreras (2002) argues that the notion of a critical intellectual, as proposed by Giroux, is therefore a somewhat utopian conception, as it does not spell out how to become truly reflective or critical.

The reflective teaching movement emerged as a reaction to the technicist view of the teacher, that is, against the conception of the teacher as a mere consumer or applicator of knowledge produced by others. As far as the reflective teacher is concerned, he or she not only applies, but constructs knowledge by reflecting on his or her practice in order to promote professional development.

Zeichner and Liston (1996) clearly oppose the view that researchers from large scientific centers are the only holders of specific knowledge and theories about teaching. For these authors, the reflexive approach presupposes the understanding that this knowledge is not restricted to environments such as universities and research centers. In their argument, Zeichner and Liston point out that teachers have ideas, beliefs and theories that can contribute to improving teaching. As can be seen, on the one hand there are theorists who criticize teachers' knowledge on the grounds that it is not based on research into teaching; on the other there are those who reinforce that teachers' knowledge provides a perspective for understanding teaching that researchers from outside the system ignore. Therefore, according to these authors, it is high time that traditional scientific society recognized and considered the knowledge of teachers and other professionals who work in schools.

Zeichner and Liston (1996) also postulate that one of the main aims of the reflective approach involves recognizing that teachers should have active roles in their practice. It is teachers who should set the objectives and outcomes to be achieved and also take on leadership roles in curriculum development and school reforms.

Zeichner and Liston (1996) also argue that reflective teachers should not only participate in the political and administrative decisions of the school, but also theorize about the issues of their practice. For these authors, teachers are best placed to find solutions to the problems they experience in practice. According to them, seeing these teachers as reflective professionals requires assuming that they can both point out and solve problems related to their practice. In other words, solving problems in practice also involves bringing in the knowledge that comes from experience, as Dewey (1959) puts it, or in Schon's (1983) terms, the knowledge that lies behind each teacher's actions. Zeichner (2003, p. 41) states that "the concept of the educator as a reflective agent seems to recognize the mastery *(expertise)* that exists in the practice of good teachers, what Donald Schon (1983) called "knowledge in action".

Pessoa and Sebba (2006) highlight another characteristic aspect of this movement: that of change, or at least the desire for change that reflective teaching awakens in teachers:

> The international movement for reflective training in the field of education, which began in the late 1980s, replaced the concept of the teacher as a technician, who must master basic skills in order to exercise their profession, and introduced the concept of the reflective teacher, who theorizes about teaching and must reflect on the pedagogical practice they carry out in order to be able to "change it" (Pessoa; Sebba, 2006, p. 43; no emphasis in original).

The teacher who is not "reflective" would be what the authors call a technical professional, i.e. a teacher who does not critically confront the problems in the classroom, but merely carries out commands from academic experts. In the words of Contreras (2002, p. 102),

> [the] technical teacher is the one who takes on the role of applying

> methods and achieving objectives, and his professionalism is identified with the effectiveness and efficiency of this application and achievement. It is not part of their professional practice to question the aims of teaching, but only to fulfill them effectively. This is how technical rationality establishes the figure of the *expert,* who legitimizes with his mastery of the techniques derived from scientific knowledge, and with his efficiency, those objectives that remain outside the debate for both teachers and society.

However, Pimenta (2002) warns that the application of the concept of reflective teaching can be marked by a disharmony with the theoretical foundations of the reflective movement. According to the author, this misinterpretation of the reflective movement can lead to a conception of practicality, which would lead people to think that reflection on practice is enough to build knowledge. This criticism warns that overvaluing teachers can lead them to reflect on themselves, on the problems of their practice, resulting in a process of individualism and therefore ignoring the social dimension of the reflective perspective.

Pimenta (2002) condemns this focus on individual teacher issues and claims that various theorists have criticized this interpretation of the reflective movement, because the changes that teachers can make are immediate and do not go beyond the classroom. For the author, reflective teaching, as conceived by Schon, is often not concerned with the context or social conditions that structure and influence its practice. According to Pimenta (2002, p. 24),

> [The transformation of teachers' practice must therefore take place from a critical perspective. Thus, a cautious approach to reflective practice must be adopted, to avoid the emphasis on the teacher strangely separating their practice from the organizational context in which it takes place.

Pimenta emphasizes, therefore, that the process of teacher change cannot be restricted to the classroom. On the contrary, it must reflect a change in a broader context, which must, above all, consider teaching as a "concrete social practice". The author highlights the importance of considering the political, institutional and theoretical-methodological scenarios when approaching reflective practice, so that this practice is not an individualized process disconnected from the social context in which teaching is inserted.

According to the author, the only way to avoid this is to emphasize the importance of the role of theory. Only in this way is it possible for reflection to go beyond the context of the classroom, taking in the wider social spheres and aiming for an emancipatory teaching approach aimed at reducing social inequalities (PIMENTA, 2002).

1.2 Teacher professional development

Academic training based on reflective teaching aims, among other things, to encourage and promote teachers' professional development. To this end, this conception of teaching contrasts with the traditional technicist view that teachers learn their *craft* by observing and putting into practice what they have learned in academia. Reflective training understands that training goes far beyond applying the knowledge produced in universities; on the contrary, it conceives of the teacher as a researcher of their own practice, as an individual who investigates and creates hypotheses about the events of their classroom practice.

It is therefore necessary to emphasize that the concept of professional development for language teachers, adopted in this work, goes far beyond what is envisaged by the *stricto sensu* concept of teacher training, since it requires teachers to do much more than have the linguistic or didactic knowledge to teach the content and to deal with the problems related to their practice mentioned above. In this sense, it can be said that the concept of professional development refers to a broad view of teaching and how its practice is reflected in the macro context of society. It is precisely because it has implications in other spheres that the professional and academic development of foreign language teachers has been a much-discussed aspect among theorists from various fields.

Among the aspects related to a teacher's professional development is the ability to promote changes in classroom practice. According to Zeichner and Liston (1996), teachers must both identify and solve problems related to their practice. In other words, solving problems in practice also involves bringing in the knowledge that comes from experience, as Dewey (1959) puts it, or in Schon's (1983) terms, the knowledge that lies behind each teacher's actions.

This requires teachers to take an active role in their practice (ZEICHNER AND LISTON, 1996). According to these authors, it is the teachers who must set the objectives and results to be achieved and also take on leadership roles in curriculum development and school reforms. However, personal problems such as psychic and physical disorders due to work overload, coupled with problems faced in the classroom such as indiscipline, are often cited by teachers as reasons why they are unable to bring about change in the school context, nor do they seek to develop professionally.

It can therefore be said that teachers' practice in the classroom and their willingness to seek change are influenced by a number of different personal (emotional and physical) and professional (working conditions) aspects that interfere positively or negatively in their professional practice.

> [...] teaching practice is the result of the interrelationship between two dimensions: one that integrates the subjective world of the teacher, represented by their ideas, beliefs that also encompass the affective, emotional, experiential (implicit theories), and the other objective, represented by the challenges faced in everyday family, social and school life (SAVELI, 2006, p. 96).

Therefore, the process of professional development or of changing the practice of the teacher and the school as a whole involves both personal aspects and aspects related to the context in which the teacher works which, in many cases, are not conducive to changing either the practice or the school. In fact, school tradition perpetuates old habits and makes it difficult to implement changes, especially when they are planned by bodies outside the educational environment.

However, Zeichner and Liston (1996) warn that the problems faced in the school context cannot be presented as impediments to personal and collective development. According to these authors, teachers cannot avoid the obligation to engage in a process of constant transformation, updating and improvement of their practice. In other words, teachers have an obligation to seek their own development and that of their students. In fact, teachers' professional development occurs when they feel pressured to change or feel confident enough to embark on a new pedagogical proposal:

> For a teacher to invest in making or reworking his or her proposals, he or she needs to feel under pressure in some way, either because he or she is taking the first steps in a particular field, or because his or her work doesn't meet the needs of the students (and he or she tries to improve, rather than running away), or because his or her professional security allows him or her to enjoy a surplus of energy available for innovation.
>
> In addition, the teacher needs to be willing to change method, because of the support of a group or the prospect of personal development, the realization of experiences that give him pleasure and trials that bring him new learning (CHANTRAINE-DEMAILLY, 1992, p. 155).

In the same vein, Pennington (1995) considers that the process of change occurs when teachers realize that they need to change their practice or when they see new alternatives to replace their practice and feel the desire to try them out. Therefore, professional development, with a view to changes in practice, is related to a proactive attitude towards the perception of their actions in the classroom, also taking into account the historical, social and cultural context in which this way of teaching is inserted. This means seeking conditions in which teachers can individually and collectively develop the ability to examine their practice, problematizing events with a view to changing their teaching practice and their professional development.

CHAPTER 2

CHANGING PRACTICES

CHAPTER 2 THE CHANGE IN PRACTICE

2.1 The process of change based on reflection[2]

Professional development through reflection, right from the start, requires teachers to be willing to change, because the process of changing teaching practice and the school as a whole involves both personal aspects and issues related to the context in which the teacher works. This is because school tradition perpetuates old habits, which represents a form of impediment to changes planned by bodies outside the educational sphere. These changes should, in fact, come from the teachers' own personal interpretations and theories about what really works in their school and what should form the core of their change strategies.

However, as Zeichner (2003, p. 37) warns, education reform planners have contributed to maintaining the educational *status quo*, since the measures adopted tend to maintain the profile of teachers as recipients of knowledge produced by others and as efficient applicators of practices focused on technical activities:

> There is little interest in developing educators' ability to exercise judgment in educational matters, both inside and outside the classroom, or in acquiring the willingness and ability to self-monitor that will enable them to learn from their own practice throughout their professional careers.

This movement towards professional development has not received much encouragement from political institutions. Therefore, it is an objective that must be pursued by the teacher themselves, as they are expected to take an active part *in* reflecting *on* and in their practice, both individually and collectively, with the aim of understanding, evaluating and rethinking the school reality with a view to bringing about change.

---

[2] This chapter was adapted from chapter 2 of the author's doctoral thesis, defended in 2010 (see references).

Changing one's own practice, that of another teacher or even that of several teachers in a school context, in the face of almost insurmountable resistance from these professionals and the school institution as a whole, requires abandoning routines and old practices. For this reason, theorists have tried to determine the conditions or situations that lead or "push" education professionals to implement changes in their own professional activities. According to Chantraine-Demailly (1992, p. 155), the process of changing a teacher's practice occurs when they feel pressured to change or feel confident enough to embark on a new pedagogical proposal:

> In order for a teacher to invest in making or reworking his or her proposals, he or she must feel under some pressure, either because he or she is taking the first steps in a particular field, or because his or her work does not meet the needs of the students (and he or she tries to improve rather than run away), or because his or her professional security allows him or her to enjoy a surplus of energy available for innovation. In addition, the teacher needs to be willing to change method, because of the support of a group or the prospect of personal development, of carrying out experiences that give him pleasure and of trials that bring him new learning.

For Pennington (1995), the process of change occurs when teachers realize that they need to change their own routine actions or when they see "alternatives available" to replace their practice and want to experiment with them. In line with this thinking, Zeichner (2003, p. 38) states that "qualitative changes in classroom practice will only occur when teachers understand and accept them as their own". Therefore, according to this author, the demand for change in education does not necessarily mean that real change in the classroom will occur, since teachers constantly resist changes proposed unilaterally, i.e. from the top down.

Pennington (1995) reinforces that lasting change in teacher behavior is the result of the process of experimenting with new practices and reflecting on their subsequent consequences. According to this view, the process of change or professional development takes place in spiral cycles involving the act of innovating, reflecting and adjusting knowledge about practice. This means that the alternatives that teachers experiment with and consider reflexively are gradually incorporated into their daily practice.

Pennington's (1995) view of the change process goes back to the ideas of Schon (1983) and Dewey (1959), meaning that the process of reflection must start from a problem detected in practice. According to the author, the beginning of the period of innovation is marked by concern with the *modus operandi* of the new practices adopted, such as new methodologies, procedures or materials, and with the factors that somehow interfere with this process. Then, through reflection on action, teachers become concerned with more general aspects that will result in a new understanding of the practice and a more profound change. Only once these practical issues have been mastered will teachers turn their attention to the social aspects of their work and to explaining or theorizing about their practice (PENNINGTON, 1995).

Thus, it can be said that in the context of reflective teaching, change is considered to be the consequence of a process of critical maturation about the teacher's individual practice and the institutional and social context that determines and influences their performance, i.e. change is the result of reflection. In line with this perspective, Gimenez (2005b, p. 194) highlights change as one of the challenges of the reflective approach, which, according to the author, stands out for "[...] bringing about changes in teachers' representations, beliefs and practices that could potentially contribute to intensifying their work".

However, if on the one hand the teacher's practice is subject to development through reflection on this practice and on theory, on the other hand it is immobilized by the contextual environment of teaching, which is generally not open to change. The following section will deal with the difficulties of implementing changes in school practice.

2.2 Difficulties in implementing change

According to Schon (1997, p. 87), attempts to change school reality and create the conditions for reflective practice often come into conflict with the school bureaucracy, which is organized around a model of school knowledge and, therefore, any initiative to change this organizational structure is seen as a threat by the institution. Contreras (1997 apud Pimenta, 2002, p. 27) expresses his concern that critical reflection does not go beyond the level of discourse, since school contexts are not analyzed in order to highlight possibilities for transformation.

Several studies, based on the work of Dewey (1959), have tried to examine why teachers don't engage in a systematic process of analyzing their own practice. The results of the studies mentioned by Gil (2005, p. 175), for example, conclude that "through reflection there can be slight modifications in teachers' practices, since it has been proven that the crystallized tradition of didactic practices imposes serious obstacles to change"

For Smyth (1991), the way to transform this educational reality is to get to the heart of the problem and discover the deepest roots that prevent change. Some factors have been commonly pointed out as reasons for this reality: the isolated nature of classrooms, the lack of time, the complexity of everyday life in the classroom and the anxiety that teachers feel when they are observed. This reality of teachers is reinforced by the educational system's assumption that the quality of teaching must be guaranteed by externally imposed minimum standards and by inspection and quality control mechanisms.

In addition, research in the field of education has increasingly demonstrated the influence of contextual aspects on teacher performance. A study by Spada and Massey (1992), cited by Borg (2003), reports the results of a study which showed how certain contextual factors have a great influence on the teaching of two trainee teachers. These authors observed that the good behavior of the students was a determining factor in ensuring that one of the trainees was able to put into practice what he had learned during his training in a creative way. However, the other trainee, faced with a notoriously unruly class, spent most of his time trying to control the students' behavior and was unable to continue with his lesson planning.

As the researchers mentioned above point out, it seems clear that problems experienced in the classroom, such as indiscipline, coupled with overwork and low pay, are factors that often discourage teachers from trying to improve their teaching or even seeking professional development.

Fullan (1994) argues that the educational system is fundamentally conservative and therefore more likely to maintain the *status quo* than to be transformed. According to the author, this is due to the way teachers are trained, the way the educational hierarchy is structured and the way governments treat education. Richards and Lockhart (2005) point out that different institutional contexts interfere with the roles that teachers take on in those institutions. According to the authors, there are contexts in which teachers are more autonomous and free to make decisions about course objectives, materials, assessment and teaching methods. There are other institutional settings, however, in which these decisions are made by a coordinator and the teacher is responsible for following the decisions made by others. Thus, in different educational contexts, teachers take on different roles as educators according to the institution's administrative structure, organizational culture and local teaching philosophy (RICHARDS; LOCKHART, 2005).

In addition to impediments related to the external environment such as the institution itself, teachers are often unwilling to change their pedagogical practice or their personal theories about their practice. Agreeing with Peres-Gomes (1992) when he states that reflection is a process imbued with values, symbolic correspondences, affective correspondences, social interests and political scenarios, it is possible to conclude that such a broad scope explains, in part, why it is so difficult to promote changes in the educational scene.

Another problem pointed out by Glaser and Strauss (1967 apud SMYTH, 1991) is the tension between the way teachers experience school and the way those who dictate the rules perceive school reality. Teachers are caught between two poles: on the one hand, worrying about the idiosyncrasies of the students; on the other, trying to meet the norms for group behavior in the classroom. Thus, teachers are forced to accommodate the needs of rules and regulations, even though they know that they prevent innovation.

In line with this line of thought, Van Mannen (1977) argues that teachers do not act according to informed scientific knowledge. On the contrary, their actions tend to satisfy pre-established norms as a standard of acceptable behavior. This tension is also pointed out by Saveli (2006, p. 96), who claims that teachers' decisions are subject to the pressures of the school environment, the ideology and the pattern of behavior that permeate the teacher's work context:

They can also be based on the systematic influences of their theoretical learning in training courses, or even on the first experiences they had when they started their profession; or they can be linked to the pressures of the school environment, the ideology and way of behaving of their work colleagues, or pressures from their parents, as well as from the administration.

Gimenez (2005b), for example, points out that lack of time, among other obstacles, has been one of the most frequently mentioned difficulties in implementing changes in teaching practice, since the reflective approach demands time. Perhaps this is why the "thorough consideration" (DEWEY, 1959) of a problem faced in the classroom or the implementation of research into one's own practice is faced with difficulties by most teachers. In addition to a lack of time, according to Andre (2006, p. 59), research activities require different skills from teaching, which are not always part of the teacher's repertoire:

> The teacher's day-to-day task in the classroom is extremely complex, requiring immediate decisions and often unpredictable actions. There isn't always time for detachment and an analytical attitude, as in research. This doesn't mean that teachers shouldn't have a research spirit. It is extremely

important that they learn to observe, to formulate questions and hypotheses and to select instruments and data that will help them elucidate their problems and find alternative paths in their teaching practice.

On the other hand, Zeichner and Liston (1996), ten years ago, already considered that the complicated and busy world of the classroom is no reason for teachers not to opt for changes that make them reflective professionals. These difficulties, according to them, do not justify things staying the way they are.

As emphasized by Zeichner and Liston (1996) and many other theorists, the problems faced in the school context cannot be presented as impediments to personal and collective development. Becoming reflective is directly related to the perception of the actions in the classroom, also taking into account the historical, social and cultural context in which this way of teaching is inserted. This means creating conditions in which teachers can individually and collectively develop the ability to examine their practice historically, problematizing the events, practices and structures of teaching.

Without taking away the teachers' reasoning in their constant complaints about working conditions in the educational scenario, it seems that the aforementioned pondering by the authors Zeichner and Liston (1996) is valid, when they reinforce the teachers' obligation to seek their own development as well as that of the institution. It is not up to education professionals to simply claim that this situation is out of their hands and perpetuate an extremely unworthy and unsatisfactory reality, as the Brazilian educational context can be described today.

It can therefore be concluded that the difficulty in transforming the reality of teaching is due above all to the factors that prevent change, because they are deeply rooted in the nature of the school and remain generally unquestioned. The main aim of reflective teaching is to change practices that have not produced satisfactory results. Reflecting alone, without this act being the driving force behind a process of transformation and development, would be like a sterile project that does not imply a concrete development of existing unsatisfactory realities.

The first step in the process of educating teachers to change social reality, according to Fay (1977 apud SMITH, 1991), is when teachers find ways to change the knowledge they have of themselves. This change allows them to break away from the perspective of dependence to the position of autonomy and responsibility. Knowing oneself and the context in which one lives is essential for implementing individual and collective changes.

CHAPTER 3

Reflecting on the challenges of foreign language teaching and learning

CHAPTER 3 The challenges of foreign language teaching and learning

3.1 Reflections on the challenges of the teaching profession

The rapid transformations of the so-called post-modern era, in the context of a globalized society, require teachers to have increasingly complex skills in order to adapt to the new world reality. In addition, teachers need not only to be attuned to the new technologies available on the market for teaching and learning foreign languages, but also to understand and participate in discussions about the political and social issues in which teaching takes place.

The first challenge for teachers is certainly to understand that the profession requires a constant process of personal and professional development. The reason for the constant need for professional transformation is due to the fact that new and increasingly complex challenges arise every day, requiring teachers to constantly search for effective means and strategies to deal with problems in different educational contexts. As discussed in the first chapter of this book, it is also necessary to understand that reflection on the challenges and problems of practice, as advocated by Dewey (1959) and Schon (1983), are routine steps in practice that are part of the reflective formation and professional development of teachers. In fact, reflecting on these practical problems encourages both students and teachers to constantly seek to improve or develop professionally.

This gives rise to the idea that teacher training is eternally unfinished, in other words, in a constant process of change and development. Perhaps this is why we believe that reflective training is an uninterrupted process that can never claim to be complete.

3.1.1 Reflections on the challenges faced by foreign language teachers in the public sector

The challenges faced by teachers and students in the foreign language classroom are many and varied, especially in the context of public schools: a) structural problems such as overcrowded classrooms, heterogeneous classes, indipline problems, lack of a suitable classroom/environment and lack of equipment and; b) teaching problems such as the use of outdated methodologies, poor teacher training, the adoption of outdated teaching material or material that is far removed from the students' reality, beliefs that are harmful to the learning process; c) problems of a personal nature for the student, such as lack of motivation to learn the language, cognitive or concentration difficulties; d) problems of a financial nature, such as low salaries, lack of multimedia resources and other equipment to help the learning process, as well as other consequences of the lack of social and financial recognition of the profession, such as lack of motivation to invest in further training and continuing education courses.

Bearing in mind this adverse context for the process of teaching and learning languages, the aim of this chapter is not to discuss each of these problems in detail, but simply to reflect on the challenges faced by foreign language teachers when they enter the job market, especially in the context of public schools. Specifically, the aim is to discuss some of the teacher's main concerns and also how reflective training enables teachers to be better prepared to face these problems as routine challenges in their classroom practice. The professional development of teachers means that they are better prepared to deal with transformations in the context of teaching, as well as reflecting on ways to try to get around the problems they experience in the classroom.

As explained in the previous section, the challenges faced by teachers and students are innumerable, ranging from low salaries and a precarious school environment to poor language teacher training and demotivation on the part of the students themselves. In addition to the difficulties related to students learning a foreign language, it is also important to note the difficulties teachers face in teaching, such as overcrowded classrooms, indiscipline and insecurity in the classroom, a low workload for foreign language classes and, above all, the social devaluation of the profession. All this means that teaching is seen as just an occupation and not a profession (CELANI, 2001). This reality forces teachers to take on many classes in several different schools, which demotivates them and makes it impossible for them to pursue their professional development (DE PAULA, 2010).

3.2 Overcoming the difficulties faced in everyday life in the classroom

Although the problems pointed out above are more recurrent in public education, it should be noted that the reality of teachers in private schools and higher education also suffers from some of the adverse situations that characterize that context. This section will focus specifically on the public education context. However, as mentioned above, many of the problems observed in public education are also observed in other foreign language teaching contexts.

Lima (2011) has compiled a collection entitled "English in public schools doesn't work: one question, multiple perspectives", which portrays and discusses the failure of English teaching in public schools. In one of the chapters of the book, Vilson Leffa tries to understand the reasons for this failure in the public network by pointing out some of the reasons for this reality, which the author ironically calls "scapegoats." According to Leffa, the attempt to find a supposed culprit is an attempt to know the origin of the problem and who is responsible for the situation in which teaching finds itself in the country. According to the author, there are three main reasons: a) the government, in its various forms, b) the poor training of language teachers and c) students who don't want to study (LEFFA, 2011, p. 18-23).

According to Leffa (2011), the main culprit for this situation is the government, especially at federal level. According to Leffa, the basis of this responsibility is the fact that the government's discourse on inclusion, contrary to what it sets out to achieve, ends up reinforcing the exclusion of the poor population that needs quality public education. In fact, the government's efforts have made no concrete progress in intervening and solving the country's educational problem.

With regard to the teacher's share of the blame, the author highlights their poor training, which can be as much a lack of linguistic competence as didactic skills. In addition, another fact that further compromises the teaching of English is the fact that it is often Portuguese teachers who take on the language classes to complete the workload (PAIVA, 2011, p. 33). Furthermore, even teachers who are qualified to teach language classes show a lack of motivation to seek professional development. Several studies have shown that many of these teachers are content to fill their working hours, but few seek to engage in a process of continuous training or improvement in relation to the foreign language (DE PAULA, 2010).

The third aspect, pointed out by Leffa (2011), is the lack of responsibility on the part of the students themselves, i.e. students who don't study and who place all their responsibility on the school or teacher, taking a passive and non-autonomous stance towards learning the foreign language. This passive attitude towards learning may be related to the fact that many students don't believe it's possible to learn a foreign language in public schools. In fact, several studies on beliefs that are detrimental to the process of teaching and learning languages were developed, mainly in the 1990s, which pointed out, among other things, the concept that English cannot be learned in public schools (BARCELOS, 1995, 1999; COELHO, 2006).

Leffa's (2011) argument, however, is not limited to inferring "the culprits" or the reasons for this situation, but is also concerned with seeking proposals to solve the problem. As a proposal for intervening in the problem presented, Leffa (2011) also tries to point out ways of overcoming this reality, citing as an example three possible strategies for trying to solve the problem: a) creating a cohesive class; b) establishing a common goal and c) finding the means to reach the goal (LEFFA, 2011, p. 29). According to the author, in order to make use of these strategies, it is necessary to create an atmosphere of complicity in the classroom, where teacher and students do not accuse each other, but are complicit and have common goals:

> The teacher's complicity with the students involves sharing a goal with them, which is neither the teacher's goal nor the student's goal; it is the goal of the class. It is this common goal that will resolve conflicts and make individual differences work in complementary distribution, overcoming one by one the difficulties that arise along the way. [...] Once the class is united around a common goal, the last step remains: to gather the means available in a given community to achieve the goal. In the case of a foreign language, the means are the cultural artifacts (books, audio resources, videos, etc.) and the people (teacher, colleagues, friends, etc.) who can be called upon to learn the language (LEFFA, 2011, p. 30).

Another relevant aspect for understanding the difficulty of teaching languages in public schools is the fact that these contexts are more realities than those of public schools.

The results of Guimaraes' work (2004) highlight how teaching foreign languages in private courses has a number of advantages over teaching languages in the public school system. In this sense, the results of the work by Guimaraes (2004) highlight how teaching foreign languages in private courses has a number of advantages over teaching languages in the public school system, since private language schools represent a privileged teaching reality with specialized teachers, appropriate environments, limited numbers of students and other peculiarities that help in the successful teaching and learning of foreign languages. On the other hand, in the public network, in addition to the excess of students per class and the lack of modern environments and use of new technologies, English teaching is often carried out by teachers from other areas (PAIVA, 2011).

Despite this, it is important to emphasize the need to overcome the difficulties faced in teaching practice, as argued by Zeichner and Liston (1996), and to seek to solve the problems related to teaching practice (DEWEY, 1959). In other words, the adverse context cannot be used as a justification for not tackling the problems of practice, nor is it an excuse for teachers to stop investing in their professional development. There is no doubt that reflective training and professional development are requirements, without which it is not possible to guarantee the quality of teaching, since it is only through reflection that teachers will be able to find ways to overcome the problems they encounter in the classroom.

CHAPTER 4

OPPORTUNITIES TO REFLECT ON THE TEACHING PRACTICE

CHAPTER 4 PRACTICE OPPORTUNITIES FOR TRAINEES

4. 1 SUPERVISED INTERNSHIP

Supervised internships are one of the opportunities for trainees to practice provided for in the PPC. The internship courses include reading about teaching practice, discussions on the subject, preparing internship projects and final reports, as well as observing the classes of teachers from the city's public school system and, later, the interns' experiences in these environments.

> The supervised internship is an action developed at the interface of the political-pedagogical project of the academic unit and the school in which it is carried out. It aims to get to know the real world in a work situation. It reveals itself as a space for building up the student-teacher as a subject who has mastery of their own practice and their social role. (PPC, 2011, p. 20) Thus, as well as having the objective of integrating theory and practice, the internship also aims to provide, during the training course, opportunities for reflection on the socio-political and educational context in which teaching takes place. According to the Pedagogical Project of the Letters Course (hereafter PPC) of the Federal University of Goias_Regional Catalao, the Letters professional must have their practice backed up by ethics and be committed to the socio-educational responsibility of their students.

According to the document, both majors in the Language Course, namely: Degree in Portuguese and Degree in Portuguese and English propose "the development of the internship as an investigative attitude that involves reflection and intervention in the life of the school, teachers, students and society" (PPC, 2011, p. 14).

In this way, according to the document mentioned above, the training of students in Letters seeks not only the acquisition and application of academic knowledge, but much more than this, it aims for the education provided by the course in question to somehow be able to stimulate the transformation of social reality:

> [The internship is not a practical activity, but a theoretical one, instrumentalizing teaching praxis, understood as an activity for transforming reality. In this sense, the curricular internship is a theoretical activity of knowledge, foundation, dialogue and intervention in reality, which is the object of praxis (PPC, 2011, p. 21).

To this end, teacher training courses should encourage students to think about social and political issues, specifically the social context in which teaching takes place. Issues of equity and social justice should be discussed and, above all, the focus should be on the student's social transformation, as Zeichner (2008) argues. According to the author:

> while I accept the general notion that we should expect novice teachers to be able to do the same things as experienced teachers, I think it is a mistake to try to separate issues of values, ethics and the politics of teaching from issues of technical competence and to postpone the development of ethical and moral competence until some form of technical competence has been achieved (ZEICHNER, 2008, p. 70).

Therefore, much more than developing technical skills, the internship offered during academic training should provide a teaching environment that is more likely to discuss, in a vertical way, social and political educational issues that are detrimental to the teacher's professional development process. In other words, this training should make the classroom experience a stage for broader discussions that take into account the macro context of society, including its social and political aspects.

4. 1.2 LIMITATIONS OF THE SUPERVISED INTERNSHIP

However, although the Internship was conceived with the aim of integrating theory and practice, so that the trainee can reflect on classroom practice, question educational policies, as well as propose the transformation of social reality, the way in which the subject is structured in undergraduate courses greatly compromises the objective of the subject. As instructed in the PPC for the Languages course at the Catalao Regional University:

> The internship has always been identified as the practical part of professional training courses, as opposed to theory. The aim, then, is to overcome the fragmentation between theory and practice based on the concept of praxis, which points to the development of the internship as an investigative attitude that involves reflection and intervention in the life of the school, teachers, students and society (PPC, 2011, p.13).

As can be inferred from the above excerpt, one of the objectives of the However, contrary to this objective, the structure of the course *per se* separates theory from practice, assigning the internship to the final years of teacher training. As can be seen even more clearly in the following excerpt, the internship only begins at the final stage of the course:

> This project complies with *CNE/CP Resolution No. 28/2001* (CONSELHO NACIONAL DE EDUCAQAO), which provides for 400 hours to be dedicated to supervised curricular teaching internships, which should begin in the second half of the course. Thus, students who opt for one of the degrees will have to take four supervised internship courses, spread over four semesters, once they have completed 50% (fifty percent) - 256 (two hundred and fifty-six) hours - of the subjects in the Common Core and 30% (thirty percent) - 591 (five hundred and ninety-one) hours - of the subjects in the Specific Core (PPC, 2011, p. 21).

Therefore, the internship in the final stage of the course is a reality in undergraduate courses which, according to Zeichner (2008), is detrimental to teacher training, because instead of integrating theoretical and practical knowledge during academic training, it perpetuates the paradigm that has been consolidated for years in education, namely teaching conceived and structured based on the separation of theory and practice.

According to the same author, the supervised internship in the final years of any degree course does not allow students to integrate theory and practice and therefore represents as distorted a view of academic training as the view of the internship as a time to apply the theory studied in the first years of their training (ZEICHNER, 2008).

Similarly, Pereira (2008) points out that conceiving of theory and practice as watertight phases of the training process means that the internship period is marked by an artificial character that is of little significance to the trainee teacher. As Pereira (2008) argues, it is only during the internship period that the teachers take over from the head teacher for a few lessons and this brief moment is not enough to guarantee effective practical experience for the trainees.

Thus, the lack of opportunity to experience the reality of the classroom from the early years of their training represents a possible obstacle to effective teacher training. Leaving this contact with the classroom until the final stage of the course, as well as separating theoretical knowledge from practical knowledge, means restricting this productive opportunity to a brief moment at the end of the teacher's training, specifically in the short period of time allocated to the internship.

In fact, many recent graduates feel unprepared to take on a classroom, whereas graduates who already have some kind of experience in the classroom, either through voluntary internship opportunities or monitoring in private schools, seem to enjoy their training course more, as they learn the theory they will experience in their daily practice in schools right from the start.

Research into teacher training has highlighted the importance of rethinking pedagogical practice in order to integrate theory and practice from the start of academic training, as an alternative teaching proposal to the one based on the disconnection between theory and practice. In fact, some courses have tried to include hours of practical activities within the total workload of essentially theoretical subjects.

As Pereira (2008) points out, despite the emergence of new proposals for teacher training on the world stage, in the national context degree courses are still very much tied to training models based on the transmission of knowledge and teacher training. As Pereira (2008) points out, new approaches and paradigms must emerge in the educational context in order to understand teaching practice and knowledge in the classroom, as well as to rethink school content as a whole. The development of research that considers the complexity of teacher practice and knowledge, articulating theory and practice, seeks to recover the active role of the teacher in the educational process. At this point, it is necessary to think of teacher training as an approach that goes beyond traditional academic training, so that it also guarantees the personal, professional and organizational development of the teaching profession (PEREIRA, 2008).

4.2 THE LANGUAGE CENTER

In addition to the scientific initiation projects offered to students mainly in the context of Federal Universities, such as PIBIC, PIVIC, PROBEC and also initiation into teaching practice such as PIBID, the academic environment offers students and the external community a wide variety of extension projects, such as application colleges, toy libraries, sports projects and others. One of these is the **Centro de Linguas (Language Center)** extension project, registered under number 316 with the Pro-Rectory for Extension and Culture, by the Unidade Especial de Letras e Lingulstica-UAELL, from UFG, Regional Catalao, which has been running for more than 10 years and represents a project that provides undergraduate students with a professional opportunity to start practicing in the classroom.

The project has around 30 scholarship holders who, in return for the financial aid they receive from FUNAPE, the project's funding agency, teach foreign language classes to the external community as well as UFG students and staff. In addition to English courses, other languages such as French, Spanish, Japanese, German and

Libras are currently offered.

The project operates like any other language school in the city, except that there are no employment ties, since the teachers are linked to the project as scholarship holders. Apart from that, the semester courses follow the rhythm of other schools, with a registration period, evaluation period, meetings and pedagogical monitoring by the project coordinator, a position reserved for UAELL teachers.

During the semester, lectures and workshops are held to discuss the teaching methodology adopted by the Project's teachers. In addition to these group discussions, there is also individual monitoring of each teacher through observation of their lessons and reflective sessions on the teacher's classroom practice. At this time, the teacher and coordinator exchange ideas about the lesson observed, highlight the positive aspects and discuss ways of solving any problems detected. This reflective session serves to make the teacher aware of that tacit knowledge, which they often don't even know they have, but which is present, albeit unconsciously, in the solutions that professionals find to problems in their practice.

These moments of reflection on practice, as Schon (1983) and Zeichner (1996) point out, contribute to the teacher's professional development since reflection makes teachers think about and find solutions to the problems they face in their classroom practice.

4.2.1 RESEARCH INTO TEACHER PROFESSIONAL DEVELOPMENT

In addition to the reflective sessions that are part of the daily pedagogical routine of the project's teachers, the Language Center is also the scene of a collaborative research project entitled *Research into teachers' professional development* (2013-2018). This research project, which is part of the Centro de Linguas extension project, aims to carry out collaborative research with English teachers at the UFG Language Center in order to investigate whether reflective sessions on classroom practice and academic texts can promote the academic and professional development of these English teachers.

The theoretical basis used is the theory of reflective education based on the work of Dewey (1959), Schon (1983), Magalhaes (2004), Liberali (2002), Pimenta (2002), Contreras (2002), Celani (2001) and other theorists in the area of teacher education. The reflexive movement disseminated by various authors, such as those mentioned above, has highlighted the contributions of the reflexive approach to the process of teacher awareness and emancipation. The idea of emancipation goes back to the work of Freire (1996, 1987), who emphasized the importance of training with a view to a critical and change-oriented attitude.

Thus, in line with Paulo Freire's thinking, teacher training cannot be developed outside the exercise of criticality and the need to be in a constant process of evolution. Thus, by taking part in research projects such as this, students not only have the opportunity to experience the profession during their studies, but they also experience scientific initiation through this investigation. Specifically, the research in question, carried out at the Catalao Regional Language Center, aims to investigate the effects of the reflective sessions on classroom practice and on the linguistic-pedagogical conceptions of the scholarship teachers. Research into practice, as well as being a way of seeking theoretical support to understand the process of professional teacher training, represents a rich opportunity for academics to become more aware of their training and work as foreign language teachers.

FINAL CONSIDERATIONS

As discussed in the chapters of this book, the main purpose of opportunities for reflection on practice is to stimulate teachers' professional development, so that they themselves take an active role in this process of personal and professional transformation, rather than waiting for the stimulus for change to come from external sectors. However, this measure is not expected to exempt the government and the bodies responsible for quality education from assuming their role in society. On the contrary, reflective training aims precisely to propose discussions about teacher training, so that teachers and trainers are aware of their role as social agents responsible for multiplying these ideas, as well as demanding that higher authorities fulfill their functions, including guaranteeing quality education for all.

The process of teacher professional development requires intervention measures, both through research aimed at finding possible contributions to alleviating the gaps that still permeate teacher training courses and through public policies aimed at promoting educational development at national level.

In this way, reflection on teaching practice, both during the internship and in the classroom at the Language Center, allows teachers to better understand the challenges and demands of the profession, as well as to find their own solutions to the problems detected in the classroom. It is worth remembering that this process of reflecting on routine problems in the classroom and attempts to resolve these issues promotes changes in teaching practice and, consequently, the teacher's professional development. In other words, teacher training is continuous and can never be considered complete, because every day we need to acquire new knowledge in order to improve our classroom practice and, therefore, our professional development as teachers.

References

ANDRE, M. E. D. A. Research, training and teaching practice. In: ANDRE, M. E. D. A. (Org.). *O papel da pesquisa na formacao e na pratica dos professores*. Campinas, SP: Papirus, 2006. p. 5570.

BARCELOS, A. M. F. A cultura de aprender linguas (Ingles) de alunos graduantes de Letras. 1995. 200 fl. Dissertation (Master's in Applied Linguistics) - Institute of Language Studies, University of Campinas, Campinas-SP, 1995.

The culture of learning languages. In: ALMEIDA FILHO, J. C. P. (Org.). *O professor de língua estrangeira em formagao*. Campinas: Pontes, 1999.

BORG, S. Teacher cognition in language teaching: a review of research on what language teachers think, know, believe and do. *Language Teaching,* n. 36, p. 81-109, 2003.

CELANI, M. A. A. Teaching foreign languages: occupation or profession? In: LEFFA, V. J. (Org.). *The language teacher:* building the profession. Pelotas: Educat, 2001.p. 21-40.

CHANTRAINE-DEMAILLY, L. Models of continuing education and strategies for change. In: NOVOA, A. (Org.). *Osprofessores e a suaformagao.* Portugal: Dom Quixote, 1992. p.139-158.

COELHO, Hilda Henrique. Is it possible to learn English at school? Teachers' beliefs about teaching English in public schools. In: BARCELOS, Ana Maria Ferreira; VIEIRA ABRAHAO, Maria Helena. (Org.) *Crengas e ensino de linguas:* foco no professor, no aluno e na formacao *de* professores. Campinas, SP: Pontes Editores, 2006. P. 125-142.

CONTRERAS, J. *The autonomy of teachers.* Sao Paulo: Cortez, 2002.

DE PAULA, Luciane Guimaraes. *A collaborative study with two female university teachers from*
english: obstacles and changes. 2010. 172 f Tese (PhD in Letters and Linguistics) _Programa de Pos-Graduação em Letras/Estudos Linguisticos, Universidade Federal de Goias, Goiania-GO, 2010.

DEWEY, J. *How we think.* Sao Paulo: Companhia Editora Nacional, 1959.

FULLAN, M. *Change forces*: probing the depths of educational reform. London: The Falmer Press, 1994.

FREIRE, P. *Pedagogy of autonomy.* Rio de Janeiro: Paz e Terra, 1996.
. *Pedagogy of the oppressed.* Sao Paulo: Paz e Terra, 1987.

GIL, G. Mapping language teacher training studies in Brazil. In: FREIRE, M. M.; ABRAHAO, M. H. V.; BARCELOS, A. M. F. (Orgs.). *Applied linguistics and contemporaneity.* Campinas: Pontes, 2005. p. 173-182.

GIMENEZ, T. Contemporary challenges in language teacher training: contributions from applied linguistics. In: FREIRE, M. M.; VIEIRA-ABRAHAO, M. H. ; BARCELOS, A. M. F. (Orgs.). *Applied linguistics and contemporaneity.* Campinas: Pontes, 2005. p. 183-202.

GIROUX, H. A. *Teachers as intellectuals:* towards a critical pedagogy of learning. Porto Alegre: Artmed, 1997.

GUIMARAES, Luciane Silva. *The teaching of pronunciation in the teaching-learning process of English as a foreign language and the communicative approach.* Brasilia, Unb, 2004, 169 p. Dissertation (Master's in Applied Linguistics). Department of Foreign Languages and Translation. University of Brasilia, DF, 2004.

LEFFA, V. Creation of goats, carnavalization and complicity: considerations on the failure of the law in public schools. In: LIMA, D. C. (Org.). *Ingles em escolas publicas não funciona:* uma questão, multiplo olhares. Sao Paulo: Parabola Editorial, 2011. P. 15-32.

LIBERALI, F. C. Agent and researcher learning in collaborative action. In: GIMENEZ, T. (Org.). *Trajectories in the training of language teachers.* Londrina: UEL, 2002. p.109-127.

LIMA, D. C. (Org.). *English in Public Schools Doesn't Work:* one question, multiple perspectives. Sao Paulo: Parabola Editorial, 2011.

LUDKE, M. The complex relationship between teachers and research. In: MARLI, M. E. D. A. (Org.). *The role of research in teacher training and practice.* Campinas, SP: Papirus, 2006. p. 27-54.

MAGALHAES. M. C. C. Language in the training of teachers as reflective and critical professionals. In: MAGALHAES, M. C. C. (Org.). *A formação do professor como um profissional crítico.* Sao Paulo: Mercado de Letras, 2004. p. 59-85.

PENNINGTON, M. C. The teacher change cycle. *Tesol Quaterly*, v. 29, n. 4, winter, p. 705-731, 1995.

PEREIRA, Julio Emilio. Educators' research as a strategy for building critical models of teacher training. In: PEREIRA, Julio Emilio; ZEICHNER, Kenneth M. A pesquisa na formação e no trabalho docente. (Org.). Belo Horizonte: Autentica, 2008.

PEREZ GOMEZ, A. The practical thinking of the teacher: the formation of the teacher as a reflective professional. In: NOVOA, A. (Org.). *Os professores e sua formagao.* Lisbon: Dom Quixote, 1992. p. 93-114.

PESSOA, R. R.; SEBBA, M. A. Y. Changes in the personal theories and pedagogical practice of an English teacher. In: BARCELOS, A. M. F.; VIEIRA-ABRAHAO, M. H. (Orgs.). *Beliefs and language teaching:* focus on the teacher, the student and training. Campinas: Pontes, 2006. p. 43-64.

PIMENTA, S. G. Reflective teacher: building a critique. In: PIMENTA, S.G.; GHEDIN, E. (Orgs.). *Reflective teacher in Brazil:* genesis and critique of a concept. Sao Paulo: Cortez, 2002. p. 17-52.

RICHARDS, J.C.; LOCKHART, C. *Reflective teaching in second language classrooms.* Cambridge: Cambridge University Press, 2005.

SAVELI, E. L. Teachers' autobiographical narratives: a way of understanding the training process. *Praxis Educativa*, Ponta Grossa, PR, v. 1, n. 1, p. 94-105, jan.-jun. 2006. Available at: <http://www.uepg.br/praxiseducativa/v1 n1artigo9 pdf>
Accessed on: Nov. 18, 2008. SCHON, D. A. *The reflective practitioner.* New York: Basic Books, 1983.
SMYTH, J. *Teachers as collaborative learners:* challenging dominant forms of supervision. Buckingham: Open University Press, 1991.

FEDERAL UNIVERSITY OF GOIAS. Special Unit for Languages and Linguistics. **Portuguese Language Course:** Political Pedagogical Project for the Language Course, 2011. Catalao, 1993. Available at :
https//letras.catalao.ufg.br/up/508/o/PPC_Portugu%C3%AAs_e_Ingl%C3%AAs.pdf Accessed on: 14-06-2017.

VAN MANNEN, M. Linking ways of knowing with ways of being practical. *Curriculum Inquiry*, v. 6, n. 3, p. 205-228, 1977. Available at: <http://links.jstor.org/sici?sici=0362-84%281977%296%3A3%3C205%3ALWOKWW%3E2.0.CO%3B2-K> Accessed on Nov. 3, 2007.

ZEICHNER, K. M. Training teachers for student-centered education: possibilities and contradictions. In: BARBOSA, R.L.L. (Org.). *Formação de educadores:*

desafos e perspectivas. Sao Paulo: Editora Unesp, 2003. p. 35-56.

ZEICHNER, K. M.; LISTON, D. P. *Reflective teaching*: an introduction. New Jersey: Lawrence Erlbaum Associates, 1996.

About the author

Luciane Guimaraes de Paula has a doctorate in Letters and Linguistics from the Federal University of Goias (2010), a master's degree in Applied Linguistics from the University of Brasilia (2004), a degree in English Language and Literature of Expression in English from the Federal University of Uberlandia (1999) and a bachelor's degree in Law from the Catalao Higher Education Center (2016).

She has worked in Higher Education for over fifteen years. She worked at UNICALDAS as a teacher from 2001 to 2004, then passed the competition for the State University of Goias, being assigned to the city of Morrinhos_GO, where she worked from 2004 to 2010. Then, in 2010, she was approved in a new competition for the position of adjunct professor at the Federal University of Goias, Catalao Region, to work as a professor of English and English-language literature at the Special Unit of Letters and Linguistics_UAELL, where she has worked ever since.

She currently coordinates the Language Center, UAELL Extension Project and also the Research Project entitled *Research on the Professional Development of Teachers*, carried out with the teachers of the Language Center. Her areas of expertise include English Language and Literature, Applied Linguistics, Language Teaching and Learning, Language Teaching Methodology and Reflective Teacher Training.

MIX
Papier aus verantwortungsvollen Quellen
Paper from responsible sources
FSC® C105338

Printed by Books on Demand GmbH, Norderstedt / Germany